A College Primer

An Introduction to Academic Life for the Entering College Student

John T. Kirkpatrick

Rowman & Littlefield Education
Lanham • New York • Toronto • Oxford
2004

This title was originally published by ScarecrowEducation.
First Rowman & Littlefield Education edition 2006.

Published in the United States of America
by Rowman & Littlefield Education
A Division of Rowman & Littlefield Publishers, Inc.
A wholly owned subsidiary of The Rowman & Littlefield Publishing Group, Inc.
4501 Forbes Boulevard, Suite 200, Lanham, Maryland 20706
www.rowmaneducation.com

PO Box 317, Oxford, OX2 9RU, UK

Copyright © 2004 by John T. Kirkpatrick

British Library Cataloguing in Publication Information Available

Library of Congress Cataloging-in-Publication Data

Kirkpatrick, John T., 1954–
  A college primer : an introduction to academic life for the entering college
student / John T. Kirkpatrick.
    p. cm.
  ISBN 1-57886-139-X (pbk. : alk. paper)
  1. College student orientation. I. Title.
LB2343.3.K53 2004
378.1'98—dc22

2004006330

♾™ The paper used in this publication meets the minimum requirements of
American National Standard for Information Sciences—Permanence of
Paper for Printed Library Materials, ANSI/NISO Z39.48-1992.
Manufactured in the United States of America.

*For Eleanor, Blythe, Grace,
and, of course, Rose*

CONTENTS

PREFACE

Many years ago, I joined my colleagues in the Office of the Dean of the College to serve in support of the work of faculty and students. The office was located in one of the oldest buildings on campus. Though stately in its presence, the building was worn by the legions of faculty and students who passed through its halls over the years. A small dome capped the ceiling of a rear entrance. The dome was dingy and tarnished, although age had not betrayed its original elegance. Some glass at the top was barely visible through soot and grime. Years of neglect were apparent. Office colleagues and I summoned a crew from Buildings and Grounds to have a look. Weeks passed and the crew began a restoration of the small dome. Dirt was removed, paint was stripped, moldings and ironwork were repaired and, yes, thick plate glass in its ceiling was cleaned and polished. Fresh enamel then was brushed upon the woodwork of the restored dome. Today, natural light bathes its design. Many say it shines.

I can't be certain of the special meaning the dome held for the architect. He passed away long ago. The dome resides there still; beauty and light in a small place. Metaphor is a human construction, an expression of a longing to share meaning with others. It just may be that the abiding genius of the small dome lay in what it so wonderfully beholds from high atop the entrance ceiling: college. Beauty and light in a small place.

ACKNOWLEDGMENTS

I am immensely grateful that so many colleagues offered insights and editorial suggestions as I worked upon this project. Rest assured, true to form, they were not always in agreement on its merits. They are a distinguished group of scholars from across the disciplines: Janet Aikins, David Andrew, Patricia Bedker, Robert O. Blanchard, Clifford Brown, Gary Cilley, Ellen Cohn, Cheryl Joy Daly, Richard Desrosier, Jeffry Diefendorf, Kurk Dorsey, Ellen Fitzpatrick, John Freear, Robert Gilmore, Peter Haebler, Ned Helms, Robert Henry, Grover Marshall, Donald Melvin, Robert Mennel, Susan Mennel, Cari Moorhead, Georgeanne Murphy, William Murphy, Melville Nielson, Jan Nisbet, Joseph Pace, Stuart Palmer, Charles Putnam, John Rouman, Mark Rubinstein, Judith Spiller, B. Thomas Trout, James Tucker, Paul Verrette, Neil Vroman, and Sally Ward. They are products of the finest colleges and universities in the world. The generosity with which they shared their experience in academic life is no surprise. It defines them *and* the special place they work. I thank them all.

Susan Dumais was wonderfully helpful in the loan of her editorial and stylistic talents. This small book is a product of her fine efforts. I am thankful, as well, for the support of Dean Marilyn Hoskin and the College of Liberal Arts at the University of New Hampshire. I owe a great deal to her and the College.

I thank Thomas Koerner and Cindy Tursman of ScarecrowEducation. They believed in the project and worked tirelessly to bring this book to press. The entire team at ScarecrowEducation was a delight to work with.

My wife, Peg, was a full partner to this project and I was fortunate to have her companionship. Her insights into college life are found within these pages as well.

INTRODUCTION

My father earned a degree in engineering from Lehigh University. My mother did not go to college. Since my father traveled a great deal when I was young, it fell largely on my mother to explain that going to college was a necessary element of the good life. She was raised among the steel mills around Pittsburgh during the depression. As an adult, she still spoke of most things in the hackneyed but rich language of her youth. "Don't go to college and you'll end up a rumdum or a noodnik." Not wanting to be either, I chose to go.

At the time, I sensed that my mother subscribed to the value of formal education for the possibility it promised in life. Much effort was expended in getting in to college, but I had little notion about what to expect once there. She had no experience of her own to lend, so details about college life were sketchy at best. Not to worry, she assured me, it would all work out in the end.

It did, of course, and I have spent the better part of my life on a college or university campus. The gaps in my mother's wisdom were filled gradually with personal experience in the academic world, but college was not always an easy place to navigate. The absence of a good guide to the academic world made the journey more harrowing than it otherwise might have been.

This is a small book about a complex social institution with an even more complicated culture: college. It is intended primarily for the entering student who, like me thirty years ago, may have little idea what to expect. This book may be useful to others, too. High school sophomores and juniors will find some helpful direction as they plan their high school studies in preparation for college. Teachers, guidance counselors, parents, and college advisors might use it to support their work with college-bound students. Getting ready to begin college calls for the entering student to imagine a sense of place and what one will be expected to do once there. The scarecrow in L. Frank Baum's *The Wizard of Oz* immediately understands his intellect upon the conferral of a diploma. In truth, college is where most of the rest of us come to a similar reckoning. It is a rarified place where magic can be found, but first one must understand how life within its borders proceeds.

The book's point of view is of the professoriate, as it should be. So much in the way of college orientation material is presented from a student's perspective. This is not altogether a bad practice, but a student is better served by learning about college from those who are its longtime residents: the faculty. After all, the veteran traveler knows that the inhabitants of a faraway place are the truest sources of its riches and mysteries. So it is with getting situated in academic life. Listen to and watch closely the faculty, those blessed to live their lives within college environs.

I do not pretend to speak for all colleagues at every college and university. Think of this book as a collection of personal essays and its narrative voice as a tale told by one with an enduring affection for college as a place where great and curious minds assemble, if only to press the boundaries of the human imagination. I have lived in such a place. I know its lore, its triumphs and failures, its treasures and its poverties. I love it still, and there is comfort that I am not alone.

THE ADMISSION

Like it or not, gaining admission to college is a competitive undertaking. Each year, college and university deans of admission evaluate and rank the achievements of thousands of candidates who aspire to enter college. Criteria for admission vary among colleges and universities, but there are common factors that weigh upon admission decisions. Standardized test scores, class rank, and program of study in secondary school are among the more important elements of a candidate's portfolio. Obviously, the higher the first two, the more attractive the candidate. Candidates would be well advised to prepare prudently for standardized tests and to aim high in graded coursework across the high school curriculum. Competition for admission is formidable, and colleges and universities use such measures to rank a candidate's abilities against others.

Program of study pursued and completed in secondary school is equally important. Mathematics, history, English, science, and foreign language should form the core of formal high school study. Most colleges and universities expect a minimum of three years in each area, but candidates should pursue four years in some subjects to demonstrate their prepa-

1

ration for college study. Breadth and depth of one's knowledge are crucial not only to admission but to college coursework as well. The successful candidate plans accordingly.

Accomplishments outside the classroom also are weighed in admission decisions. Achievements in the arts and athletics speak of a candidate's commitment to mastery of talent over the long term. Participation in clubs, social activities, and community service demonstrate one's understanding of the responsibility to a public beyond the self. A record of involvement in activities outside the classroom surely improves the odds for admission, but it rarely offsets inattention to standardized tests, academic record, and course of study. It is best to think of extracurricular achievement as a reflection of the fuller self and not the sole substance of one's presentation to the dean of admission. As a rule, the demonstrated application of intellect in coursework remains the more revealing mirror of academic prowess and promise.

The choice of the appropriate college or university for you is a very personal one. Size, location, cost, and campus amenities understandably will influence your thinking. Some students even consider the rankings of athletic teams or the lure of an active social life. The academic program, however, should always be at the heart of your decision. Carefully review the academic offerings of a college or university and assess how well they fit with your

strengths and aspirations. Here your guidance coun-
selor or a favorite teacher can assist you to find a
proper fit. One day, you will appreciate just how much
pride they take in your efforts to prepare for college
study.

Some high school seniors start their college career by choosing a local community college. Community colleges offer two-year degree programs.
Often, graduates of such programs then transfer to
colleges and universities offering four-year degrees.
Community college can be a good choice for students who desire a smaller setting closer to home in
order to ease their transition to the college environment. Moreover, much of the coursework completed
in a two-year program will count toward a degree at
a four-year institution.

Perhaps for most readers, you already have ac-
cepted your invitation of college admission. Your
college application was submitted and reviewed fa-
vorably. You now have in hand an acceptance letter,
your official visa, allowing you at long last to embark
upon the journey through the academic world. Well
done! Congratulations are in order. By all means, take
pride in your achievement, but be humbled by the
knowledge that others, for various reasons, do not
have a similar letter.

Now it is time to prepare anew for entrance into
college. College is a place unlike any other, and finding
your way in the academic world will require your full
attention. True, your efforts to date have carried you

to the college gates, but you now must prepare for the world inside. Put away your accolades. It is no sin to refer back to them, of course. They are important parts of your biography, and only venial harm is done when reliving past glories. Do not rest comfortably on such laurels. A new world awaits, and you are among its newcomers. Those who enter with you carry equally impressive credentials. Once in college, few will be impressed with how you arrived. More will be interested in how you comport yourself while there. Be sure to understand why that is, and you will be well positioned to begin your journey.

THE HISTORY

At first blush, college can appear an imposing place to be. Its residents, however, know well the rhyme and reason of its long life. There is poetry in the very idea of college and a logic to its longevity in the course of human affairs.

College, or the academy, is an exalted place of higher learning. Plato was at its beginning. While a brilliant thinker and orator, his teaching methods eventually were seen to be prescriptive and dogmatic. Those who followed him grew impatient and soon would expand discourse to include free and open inquiry. The ancient Greeks labored to organize the learned to advance the arts, letters, and the sciences. Prior civilizations paid equal homage to learning, but the ancient Greeks defined it as a freestanding virtue and gave it form. In time, the "academe" became a lively marketplace of ideas. Intellect was its currency. Fiercely acquisitive merchants of the mind traded openly within its halls.

College owes its remarkable longevity, from Plato's time to the present, to an enduring human allegiance: there must be a place in the social order where knowledge is created and transmitted across generations. This is a useful meditation, one as important to you and your time as it was to Plato and his. Some entering students believe that the academic world begins and ends with them. Wiser students know this to be folly, for college does not suffer well the self-centered. The proper tonic for the misguided is historical consciousness, so indulge generously before your arrival. The history of college as a human institution of higher learning is long and storied. Knowing something of its development provides perspective, helping you to understand the evolution of your new world and the inertia that propels it.

From Plato's time though the Middle Ages, the academy's faculty would assemble anywhere, often in religious sanctuaries, and students would congregate around them, living in whatever available space could be found. The permanent residence of the academy in a defined space, or campus, would not develop until the twelfth and thirteenth centuries. It was then that the academy took root in set places where faculty and students worked and lived together.

Campuses began to sprout throughout Western Europe in the fourteenth century, most notably in England, France, and Italy. Oxford, Cambridge, the Sorbonne, Cologne, and Padua, among others, acquired buildings and formed communities of resident scholars who would serve as mentors to the students they attracted. Teaching was the core mission at such places, the stock of existing knowledge passed from one generation to the next. Theology, medi-

cine, and law were early areas of university instruction. Renaissance thinkers, however, encouraged
teaching across a much broader range of disciplines.

As they grew in size and complexity, these
assemblies of scholars and their young charges defined themselves as universities, from the Latin, "uni-
versitas," which loosely translates as "everything
under the sun." Their growth brought subdivisions
within them, separating into departments of faculty
who shared the same passion and interests across
the intellectual landscape. Some scholars took history as their master, others literature, mathematics,
aesthetics, ethics, religion, science, and so on. Faculty expected a breadth of knowledge in each other,
but recognized that each colleague was entitled to
join like-minded scholars to plumb a chosen area of
specialized study. These divisions and the principle
behind them prevail in college to this day.

Over the centuries, university faculty designed
elaborate curricula. A curriculum is a prescribed program of formal study that scholars believed defined
the substance of the educated mind. The completion
of study in core areas of knowledge was necessary
to earn the award of a university degree. In turn, the
degree would signify mastery and high achievement
among those who held it.

While teaching proved to be a durable and worth-
while mission of universities in the Middle Ages and
during the Renaissance, there soon developed another, equally dramatic mission that would serve quite

compatibly as teaching's twin: research. Scholarly curiosity was its source. An active agency in testing beliefs about the physical and social worlds seemed to be a sensible way to advance knowledge, and research became a reliable vehicle to discovery. Royal societies throughout Europe were the places where research first appeared, but universities soon embraced it as vigorously.

Great German institutions from the seventeenth through nineteenth centuries, such as the University of Heidelberg and Humboldt University in Berlin, were early champions of research. Structured laboratories in the physical and life sciences developed on their campuses to test hypotheses molded from existing knowledge. Scientific methods were engineered, technologies developed, and measurements meticulously recorded and replicated in order to judge the merits and limits of theories sprung from the minds of university scholars. Through research, new knowledge could be created systematically, with more certainty and with accelerated speed. Disciplines outside the sciences embraced research as well. Existing canons in literature, aesthetics, and religion were examined critically and recast when new ideas about the human condition emerged. The focus on research spread to America and its universities, and found hospitable homes at Johns Hopkins and other institutions. Colleges and universities could hardly contain the euphoria.

The twentieth century brought expansive growth to the academy. Colleges and universities grew in number and in size. In the latter half of the century, concerted efforts to recruit faculty and students of both genders and of all races and ethnicities enriched scholarship immensely. Multiple points of views, diverse cultural legacies, and the resulting challenges to conventional thought led to remarkable developments in nearly all disciplines. Colleges and universities recognized that sound teaching and research were served better by an open, not restricted, invitation to all who harbored scholarly will and talent. That is why the modern academy draws the sharpest of minds to its halls. All with proven ability are welcome.

Today, teaching and research form the lifeblood of colleges and universities throughout the world. Some may place greater emphasis on one over the other, but both enjoy a happy relationship on most campuses. To push the boundaries of knowledge and to do so in the company of those still learning are the mainstays of college. Centuries may have passed since the academy imagined by the ancient Greeks, but the marketplace remains. Today, it is a livelier place than they could have ever dreamed. When you enter, be prepared for the bustle of intellectual trade in the modern world. It absolutely hums.

THE PROFESSORIATE

A distinguished senior colleague once told me that he came to understand early in his career the difference between the high school teacher and the college professor. A jazz pianist, he had been both. The difference, he said, is that the high school teacher is driven by a passion for teaching. The college professor is impassioned by a pure love for the discipline.

This is a stark contrast, but in it there is great truth. Through your years of formal education, if you were lucky, you were mentored by those with complete dedication to your intellectual and social development. You were pushed to learn even when you resisted. Primary and secondary school teachers exerted a great deal of control over your whereabouts, activities, and progress. One can hardly argue with such a practice. After all, your college admission is a product of your hard work *and* their supervision.

Now, however, it pays to know that college professors expect much more of you in your own higher education. So complete is their devotion to their disciplines that they seldom are willing to enslave themselves to supervision. Think of the difference between the hen and the mother duck. The hen scurries to keep her young charges within a distance of proper oversight, herding the stray chick to stay within her brood. The mother duck, on the other hand, walks stridently in the lead. Pity the errant duckling who fails to fall in behind her. The college professor is decidedly of the duck variety.

High school and college are very different in their academic demands. College is not simply a continuation of high school, like grade thirteen (see table 1). It is structured to place a much heavier burden of responsibility on *your* shoulders. College faculty understand that this is a difficult adjustment for you to make, but adjust you must. Consider the many differences between the high school and college academic environments.

TABLE 1: HIGH SCHOOL VS. COLLEGE

DIFFERENCES	HIGH SCHOOL: WHERE YOU ARE	COLLEGE: WHERE YOU WILL BE
instructors	*teachers*	*professors*
guidance	*mentors seek out students*	*students must seek out mentors*
class schedule	*classes meet daily*	*classes meet one to three times per week*
class size	*20 to 50*	*15 to 500*

TABLE 1 (continued)

note-taking	*encouraged*	*absolutely necessary*
examinations	*frequent*	*periodic: sometimes only two to three per class per semester*
reading assignments	*moderate*	*heavy*
writing assignments	*moderate*	*heavy*
homework	*daily and graded*	*weekly and largely ungraded*
grading criteria	*effort and progress are often considered*	*mastery of material is* <u>*the*</u> *criterion*
parents	*there*	*not there*
time management	*managed for you*	*managed by you*

All of this is to emphasize that you will be treated by your professors as one who clearly wants to be where you are, in college. You snooze, you lose, and few professors will be inclined to wake you. The obligation of college is to put in your way the great minds and ideas of our times. Do not, through inattention, miss the precious opportunities to meet both.

Understanding how and why your professors got to "be" professors is a first step in your adjustment to the college environment. See the world through their eyes and you will appreciate how dearly they cherish their scholarly work. College and university faculty have spent years in formal study after receiving their undergraduate degrees. Law school involves three years of postgraduate study and medical school requires four. The award of the Ph.D. usually involves five or more years of formal study. It is an arduous undertaking of scholarly training and ends after rigorous examinations by established scholars in the field and the completion of a lengthy dissertation of original scholarship. No wonder only the passionate survive.

Adding to this often grueling endeavor is the young scholar's effort to win an appointment to a college or university faculty. Competition is stiff. Candidates are chosen through exhaustive national searches for the best and the brightest. Once appointed, faculty enjoy promotion through the ranks of the professoriate after thorough reviews of their ongoing teaching and scholarship conducted by panels of accomplished peers. If you are sobered by the intensely critical posture of faculty who review your work, know that it pales in comparison to the posture assumed by faculty when assessing each other's work. The gold braid on faculty caps and the three velvet stripes worn on their academic robes are emblems of intellectual perseverance in a necessarily critical world.

Faculty understand that criticism is a vital ingredient of scholarly work. If there is value in a new idea, it must withstand scrutiny. You also must come to expect and, indeed, embrace close scrutiny of your work once in college. Faculty will push you beyond what you may regard as personal limits. They do so not out of a mean-spirited predisposition toward you. Rather, they do so in order to strengthen the qualities of intellect demanded of you after you graduate. You must be prepared better than you are now. College faculty regard this as a heady summons of responsibility, to you and to the future that one day you will help to shape. So, rest assured that faculty will expect you to follow their lead. Accept this often not-so-gentle instruction. Through your studies, college faculty will reveal to you special gifts that you alone possess and that you are duty-bound to share when you leave them. Then you must move forward without them. Faculty want very much for you to do so with strength of mind, sureness of foot, and courage of heart.

Remember that college faculty are driven by insatiable appetites for creating new knowledge and passing on what is known about the world to a new generation. Their scholarly work is a boundless obsession. The hours in a day are seldom able to contain it. Faculty write and create endlessly, all the

while redrawing the edges of human knowledge. Recognize the good fortune of being in their company.
When in college, follow them closely and respect-
fully. Engage yourself thoroughly in scholarly study
and learn what lessons they offer you. College faculty know full well that your time to lead will come
soon enough.

THE DEGREE

Colleges and universities are entrusted with the responsibility to award the bachelor's degree to those who demonstrate proficiency in an established curriculum. This is not a democratic process where you will have an equal voice in what constitutes mastery of knowledge. Faculty determine its constitution. Recognize that college is the "major league" of intellectual life. Your achievements will be judged by demanding managers, the faculty.

A college degree is earned. It is not purchased, finagled, or the product of hard work alone. To receive the degree, you must demonstrate clear mastery of material across the disciplines, completing successfully a comprehensive curriculum designed by faculty to embody the educated mind of the twenty-first century. It will not be easy, nor should it be. Remember that faculty are obligated not only to develop your talents, but also to signal to others upon conferral of the degree that you are ready to assume high-level responsibilities in the world at large. Faculty would be remiss in their duty to the wider society if they gave the world a civil engineer who failed calculus or a nurse who had only a loose grip on human anatomy and physiology. Ask yourself if you would cross a bridge built by such an engineer or undergo surgery assisted by such a nurse. Of course not, and that is why faculty will grade your work with high standards in mind. You must prove yourself worthy before they will allow you to leave them with degree in hand.

There are many different types of degrees: bachelor of arts, bachelor of science, bachelor of fine arts, bachelor of music, and others. More often than not, the type of degree depends upon the discipline of your chosen major. Generally, you need not worry about this choice yet. Many college students enter with only a vague notion of what they would like to pursue. Accordingly, first-semester courses will be fairly tightly assigned no matter what you pursue in later years of college study. The initial academic advisor assigned to you will see to it that the selection of first-semester courses will start you off well.

A college degree program is about both breadth and depth of knowledge. Most colleges require you to complete a core set of courses, often called general education requirements. These requirements address breadth of knowledge. All students must successfully complete required coursework, notably in writing, mathematics, foreign language, literature, the sciences, the fine and performing arts, culture, history, and philosophy. These are not subject areas irrelevant to your higher education. On the contrary, they are essential elements of studious preparation for life in the modern world. In any case, do not quarrel with these requirements. There is no getting around them. If you fail to see their relevance now, you will in time.

A major sees to depth in your degree program. Think of your major as an intensive area of study. You will start with introductory-level coursework, move through the intermediate level, and advance as a senior to upper-level seminars reserved for the accomplished student in the field. In the major, you take a considerable number of courses, usually about ten, and its structure is designed to lead to mastery of a single field. Once you demonstrate mastery in that field, the tools you used to do so will serve you to master others of your choosing later in life.

You should select a major based upon two criteria: your passion and your strength. One can love something and, frankly, be weak in aptitude. Conversely, one can despise something but be quite good at it. Do not choose a major if either of these maxims apply. Instead, find a major that at once fulfills a passion *and* plays to your strength. Time will help you to find a major that reflects a proper balance between the two. There is no hurry. Most colleges will not require you to declare a major until the end of your second year of study. In the meantime, search prospective majors with these two criteria in mind. Worry less about what you will "do" with that major upon graduation. Consider instead its meaning and value to you, and its relationship to the special promise you hold. After reflection and good counsel from your mentors, you will know when and what to declare as a specific major of intensive study.

A description of a college degree program would not be complete without some mention of grades. As in high school, they are measures of proficiency ranked against your peers. You do not have a say in their award. Apply yourself and certainly make the effort to monitor your standing with faculty in any given course. Be sure to understand, however, that the sobering responsibility to assess your proficiency is theirs alone. Faculty take this responsibility seriously and so should you. Hard work and diligence are givens on your part, but they may not always produce the grade you desire. Natural aptitude plays a role. Put another way, expect to earn higher marks in some courses than in others. You will find competition for high grades tougher than you did in high school. Your college classmates are as gifted as you, will work as hard, and represent a range of aptitudes across the disciplines. Stay focused, remain dedicated, be actively engaged and you are sure to find your game.

Cumulative grade point average (GPA) and class rank are lasting benchmarks of your abilities. Make both as high as you possibly can. You must drain every drop of your energies to do so. It will take time, however, to perform well. If you are like most college students, your grades will improve steadily over your four years. A modest goal during your first semester is a 2.50 GPA out of a maximum of 4.00.

You may think that this bar is set too low, but it is not. You have significant academic adjustments to make as you begin college and the demands of college work are like no other that you have encountered to date. Earn a 2.50 or better during your first semester and you will be well positioned to graduate with honors. Importantly, reaching that mark in your first year shows faculty and deans that you have the right stuff to continue.

THE STRUCTURE

A t this point, your understanding of the structure of college is probably a product of contact with the dean of admissions, glossy college publications, websites, and what is portrayed in movies and television shows. You even may have picked up something about the order of college life from older siblings or friends. There is no substitute for actually being there yourself, however. In preparation for your arrival, a simple roster of who's who may be useful.

College and university presidents are nearly always highly accomplished scholars with impressive track records in their fields and in academic leadership. They oversee the general operation, fiscal health, and academic integrity of their institutions. A president's job is not an easy one. With so many talented people in their fold, more than one president has compared the job with herding cats. Be that as it may, the president is the one responsible for the overall direction of an institution of higher learning and tending to its reputation. You'll know who they are. Everyone on campus calls them "president." They are also the ones leading the processions at academic ceremonies.

Serving under the president is the provost, vice president of academic affairs, or dean of faculty.

Depending upon the size of a college or university, these titles are used interchangeably. Larger institutions generally have provosts, the mid-sized have vice presidents, and smaller ones have deans of faculty. In all these cases, the title conveys responsibilities of a chief academic officer. They are directly responsible for the vitality of the curriculum and the faculty recruited to teach and conduct research. Their charge is to make certain that an appropriate environment exists in order for faculty and students to proceed with their proper work.

You may have only minimal contact with your president and provost, but you most certainly should know your college dean. A dean is the head of a large group of faculty that represent many discrete disciplines tied together by their membership in a college. The college dean is usually at work with the president, provost, other deans, and department chairs on ways to strengthen the twin missions of teaching and research. A small college will have one dean. A large university will have several, owing to the fact that a university is an aggregation of many separate colleges, often liberal arts, business, education, health, engineering, and the sciences. At many universities, you are admitted as a first-year student in one of its colleges, although once you are there, you usually can transfer from one college to another depending upon your developing interests and performance. Often, a dean will have one or more associate deans working within the office. The associate dean is the person who oversees the progress you make in your degree program. It is not such a bad idea to meet with the associate dean from time to time to discuss your academic progress and plans.

The department chair heads a collection of faculty, known as a department, in a specific discipline, joined by their love for a subject area. History, psychology, English, physics, chemistry, nursing, engineering, business, and many others all are organized into separate departments. A collection of similar departments is organized as a college and a set of colleges as a university. You get the idea. Department faculty meet regularly as a group to discuss teaching assignments, their scholarship, committee work, and plans for the future of the department. The department chair leads these discussions as well as oversees the progress of scholarship among department faculty. The chair in your chosen major is a helpful resource to you on matters of direction in your major.

Your president, provost, dean, and department chair are scholars you will want to know, even if your interactions with them are glancing ones. The faculty, however, you *must* know, since they serve as the stewards of your higher education. Faculty hold specific ranks within the professorate: assistant professors are the most junior of faculty, associate professors are at mid-career, while the title of full professor is bestowed only upon the most senior and accomplished of the professoriate. Faculty rise through these ranks only after clear demonstration of outstanding teaching ability and in honor of recognized scholarship in their fields. Senior faculty are revered in academic life, and a good deal of respect accrues from their enviable achievements. Honor them as others in the academy do. They earned the courtesy through their demonstrated powers of intellect.

There are other offices in the academy: vice presidents of finance, administration and research, deans of student affairs, registrars, directors of business services, financial aid, alumni affairs, and the like. Their work also contributes mightily to the vitality of a college or university. The president, provost, dean, chair, and the faculty are the ones upon whom you should focus your attention, however. They work diligently to shape your college education. If the hours in the day are short and you must choose to meet with only one of them, the wise choice is the faculty. The structure of college may appear to be hierarchical, but the seasoned college or university president knows that faculty are the driving force of intellectual life on any campus. Normally, academic institutions are judged by the distinction of their faculty and the caliber of students under their wing.

THE CULTURE

Culture is an amalgam of all the ways in which a people connect with one another. Culture includes language, music, art, common habits, customs, traditions, shared values, spirituality, styles of dress, and all other human creations that define a sense of place. Think of all of these elements as they circulate throughout your hometown and mark its character. Now move your thoughts to what college culture may bear.

The beauty of college is that it concentrates cultures from all over the world, assembling them in one place at one time. Art, literature, artifacts, style, and music from everywhere enjoy a comfortable residence in college. You will see, hear, and imagine things there that span the range of human existence. Be alert. The cultures of humankind will surround you and challenge what you know from your own experience. This is by design, and it speaks to what college culture is all about.

If pressed to define other attributes of college culture, three come to mind. First, college is an inquisitive culture. Exploring the unknown simply because one can is a preoccupation of college life. The human intellect is a naturally curious beast, and it is seldom quieted. Questions, always more questions.

Second, the culture of college is an acquisitive one but not in the usual way of thinking. College faculty and students are rarely impressed with the accumulation of material goods. Instead, they acquire knowledge, and ideas themselves become the products to chase and collect. You will find college faculty to be protective of the ideas they create. Ownership of ideas is a respected right in the academy. Do not be mistaken. College culture promotes the free trade of ideas, but only with proper attribution to their originators. Both poachers and poseurs are banished from the marketplace.

Third, college culture values daring and courage. The frontiers of new knowledge hold their dangers, but the inhabitants of college move fearlessly and willfully beyond the safe and secure. The risks of failure seldom impede the endless press onward into emerging territories of the intellectual landscape. Creativity, innovation, and the utter resolve with which they are applied are hallmarks of college culture and help explain why colleges and universities are powerful engines of new knowledge. As evidence, one need only look to the startling advances in art and science that flow freely from them each year or the academic affiliations of Nobel laureates, past and present.

These three attributes, inquisitiveness, acquisitiveness, and intellectual daring, define college culture. They color nearly all human interaction on campus. Sense their presence as you enter the college gates. They shape the extraordinary character of college culture.

THE FOLKWAYS

At King's College in Cambridge University, there is a large quadrangle that sits majestically in the center of campus. In it, there are no trees or flowerbeds. Instead, the space is a meticulously manicured and lusciously green lawn, bordered by paved walkways joining one end to the other. Students and visitors must be careful to stay upon the walkways. The right to trod across the grass itself is afforded only to senior faculty of the College.

This may seem like a silly rule of behavior, but adherence to its normative prescription and others like it guide much of everyday life within the campus. Folkways are customs. Think of them as informally agreed upon ways of behaving that smooth the way in which you interact with others, like shaking hands or opening doors for elders. Departure from established folkways won't earn you jail time, only a disapproving look or unpleasant rejoinder.

Any culture is laced richly with folkways. College is no different. On your campus, there may be some folkways unique to its culture. What is done at one college may not translate to another. It is highly unlikely, for example, that you will garner leers if you walk upon the grass. Nonetheless, simple powers of observation will assist you in learning the folkways on your campus. Classmates and faculty rarely tell you what they are. You are expected to rely upon cues from others about what social norms prevail on your campus. Do not worry. You will catch on quickly.

There are some folkways that are more uniformly shared across all colleges and universities. This is to say that learning them should put you in good stead no matter where you go to college. What follows is more etiquette than law, but mastery of these cultural courtesies will earn you the respect of faculty and those who work with them.

PROPER ADDRESS

Faculty should always be addressed as "Professor," Deans as "Dean," and all other college staff as "Dr.," "Mr.," or "Ms." Resist the urge to be familiar. First names are a poor choice.

ATTENDANCE

Go to class. Spotty attendance is perilous.

PUNCTUALITY

Be on time for class, seminar, and laboratory. Period.

DECORUM

The classroom environment is controlled by your professor. Do not sleep, read the newspaper, bring a meal, smoke, or gossip with classmates. A beverage like coffee or a soft drink is generally acceptable. Remove your hat, unplug your headphones, and under no circumstances should your cell phone ring. Once in class, stay there until it ends.

PREPARATION

By all means, be prepared for class. At the beginning of each term, your professors will hand out course syllabi. A syllabus is a plan of study for the course. Assigned readings, writing assignments, and examinations are matched to specific dates. These are not suggestions or otherwise negotiable. They are requirements of you. Meeting them is your responsibility.

EXTRA CREDIT

As a rule, there isn't any.

TIME

The proper management of time in college is difficult to achieve. Remember that college study requires an active engagement. Your academic work should be the centerpiece of your daily ritual. Expect to spend a minimum of six to eight hours a week in out-of-class study for each course you carry. A simple calculation clearly indicates that college work is a full-time commitment. Do not grumble about work load, at least not within earshot of faculty. Your job, social life, or extracurricular activities must never impinge upon your studies. And one more thing. Do not make holiday travel arrangements until you are certain of set times for examinations. The latter takes precedence over the former. Your grade will bear the consequence of misplaced priorities.

OFFICE HOURS

These are set hours when professors will be in their offices. Usually, office hours are specified on course syllabi. Faculty invite you to meet with them at those times to discuss almost anything. Seize the opportunity.

FACULTY CONTACT

In college, faculty contact should be cultivated, but remember that faculty are of the duck variety. You must keep yourself close to them. If you are lost, find them. They will not find you. Talk to them before or after class, during their office hours, or make an appointment. Since faculty are busy with the demands of their teaching and scholarship, make the most of your time with them. Prepare questions before you meet. Faculty are genuinely impressed by thoughtful and considerate students. E-mail is a wonderful way to engage faculty as well. One caution: e-mailing the night before an examination, the day an assignment is due, or with a conveyance of an excuse for inattention is not well received. Do not be seduced by the temptation. It suggests reckless habits of the mind *and* heart.

THE LIBRARY

The college or university library is the central hub of academic culture. All of academic life revolves around it. It is a hallowed place where the trading of ideas through written form occurs. Scholars write books and journal articles to share with others in their respective fields. The library is where such work is housed, inviting all who so desire to read it and judge its merits. You will have access to all of human knowledge within the library stacks and through its information systems. Make use of its resources. Know where it is, how it works, who among its staff can help you, and the hours it is open. There are no other places in the modern world that are as rich and as precious in human undertaking. The educated mind comes from frequent visits.

THE WEB

The information-sharing abilities brought by the digital age have transformed human communication. Computer information systems often are of the highest quality on college campuses. You will be pleasantly surprised at the speed and breadth of access to the World Wide Web, as compared to that to which you may have been accustomed. Conduct yourself appropriately when using the net. As a rule, write nothing and do not travel anywhere virtually that you would not want faculty to witness at will. Profanity, pornography, piracy, and personal insult have no place on college computer systems.

"NOBODY TOLD ME"

These words, taken together, are not a part of the college vocabulary.

Cliques

Much of your high school experience may have been circumscribed by the cliques to which you did or did not belong. College life is altogether different. Cliques are rarely in vogue on college campuses, since social exclusion can be an unintended by-product of inclusion. Do not allow yourself to be defined by any one status. Moreover, open yourself to the possibilities in others, many others. Those in college who adhere to the popularity standards of high school rarely thrive. Such standards tend to stunt the growth of college students. Exclusivity is viewed simply as bad form.

A car

A car is not necessary during your first year of study, if ever in your college career. On many campuses, first-year students are discouraged from having cars on campus. This practice is designed to focus your attention fully on acculturation to campus life. Besides, campus parking is often a nuisance. When you must leave, make use of public transportation systems.

Travel

The educated mind is anything but provincial. Faculty are utterly in love with travel, and understandably so. They are by nature an inquisitive lot and seeing places, museums, libraries, drama, research sites, and colleagues across the globe is a prerequisite of the job. Faculty also share their scholarship with colleagues at national and international professional gatherings each year. The well-traveled professor is almost always a respected one. Here, as in other matters, follow their lead. Go abroad for a year, a semester, a summer, or a week. But go.

ACADEMIC ADVICE

Rely upon no one other than faculty and academic advisors for direction in course selection, degree requirements, and choice of major. Well-intentioned roommates, classmates, and dorm staff are notoriously unreliable sources. Their counsel is built largely from hearsay and comes with considerable risk. You are better served by finding a professor or academic advisor to serve as your guide in planning your studies. Seek out an academic mentor and work at developing a relationship. Then listen to your mentor. By the way, the truly successful student has at least three. Second and third opinions are useful. Remember, however, that *you* alone will be responsible for the choices you make (see "nobody told me"). Mentors are there to help, but will not weigh in unless invited.

CAMPUS-WIDE LECTURES

In addition to coursework, college offers students the chance to hear from reputable writers, artists, scientists, political leaders, and intellectuals from around the world. Outside scholars are invited periodically to campus to give open lectures about their work. You will be poorer for the missed opportunities to hear from them. Be alert to campus postings about their visits. Their talks provide a richer texture to your college experience.

THE MORES

U nlike folkways, cultural mores are strict rules, and breaking them elicits penalties. Mores are more like laws than customs. So important are they to the well-being of a culture that formal sanctions accrue when they are breached. Think of the difference between criminal law and etiquette. Criminal offenses are transgressions of the mores. Social lapses violate the folkways. There is a substantial distinction between the two.

Once in college, you will be expected to know the mores and to abide by them. Swift punishment will come if you do not, punishment that you do not control. Almost all colleges and universities will give you two important volumes: the undergraduate catalogue and student handbook. Read both. They contain the code of conduct to which you will be held as a college student. Ignorance of its existence will serve as an unpredictable companion if you violate the code of conduct.

Like folkways, the mores on college campuses vary from one to the next. There are some mores, however, that are uniformly in place across college campuses. Know these to be true and strictly enforced.

Academic dishonesty

You must never engage in any form of deceit in your academic coursework. It is, perhaps, *the* cardinal rule of college. Faculty practice zero tolerance. In college, ideas are treated as property. Intellectual thievery is verboten and woe to the student who engages in it. Expulsion from the college gates is the imminent danger, a scarlet letter upon the chest. When in doubt about what constitutes dishonesty, consult your professors, sooner rather than later.

Material theft

What is yours is yours. What is not is not. Do not confuse the boundary between your property and that of others. Theft of any kind invites college sanctions and perhaps criminal prosecution.

Violence

Unwanted physical contact of any form also results in college sanctions and quite possibly criminal prosecution. When in any doubt about whether or not your behavior could be construed as physical or sexual assault, do not waiver from decency.

Language

Intellectual discourse takes place in an environment of free inquiry awash in civility. In college, words are tools, and their usage must always be free of malicious intent to do personal harm. College faculty and their students are obligated to engage each other in the pursuit of knowledge but to do so with respect for the dignity of each other. The profane and the hurtful generally are ostracized or worse. Sometimes, the line between the appropriate and the inappropriate can be somewhat murky. It is imperative, however, that you avoid monikers, epithets, or labels that diminish others, particularly when those terms are born of immutable characteristics. Sadly, you hear such words used in song, film, and on television. Know that this does not give you license to do the same. Civility is acquired. Practice the art while in college and you will be well served in life.

ALCOHOL AND DRUGS

The legal drinking age is twenty-one. The use of illicit drugs is proscribed by law. You will be treated as an adult by your college and in criminal court if you fail to respect the law. Rest assured that being a college student will not earn you a "get out of jail free" card. On the contrary, errant college students risk their freedom and their futures.

VANDALISM

You will come to appreciate that college faculty and students regard their campus as sacred ground. A campus' physical beauty is testament to their deep affection for it. You are a newcomer. Do not desecrate its physical or intellectual holdings in any way lest you fall precipitously from grace.

THE LIFE OF
THE MIND

Some friends argue that the challenge of the *New York Times* crossword puzzle is not what it was a quarter century ago. Clearly, they suggest, contemporary crossword composers have lost a step. Their argument is a close cousin of Mark Twain's revelation. As Twain got older, it seemed his father got smarter.

Twain and my peers, wittingly or not, point to the ongoing march of their *own* education. Life experience brings its share of valuable lessons, to be sure. The sense we make of those experiences, however, is enhanced, sometimes imperceptibly in the course of everyday affairs, by formal education. Intellect matures through structured inquiry; discovery is a product of the tenacious commitment to learn and then learn still more. In college, the seeds of knowledge are planted. Unending education over the life course surely will see to their nourishment. College will provide you with the qualities of mind, mental tools if you like, with which to order the world around you. The ability to think in the abstract; an understanding of the arts, sciences, letters, and historical context; and an appreciation of the mechanics and dynamics of human affairs will give fuller meaning to all that you encounter after you complete your college study. That college will compel you to learn for a lifetime is its most precious legacy.

You are to begin a remarkable journey. Stand ready at the college gates. Once open, those gates reveal the high resolution of the life of the mind.

THE
COMMENCEMENT

You are set to begin your formal studies in college. It is not a bad idea to go back now and reread the preceding essays. Absorb what you can before your college study commences. Once started, college is no longer a notion. It bursts like fireworks all around you.

Commencement is a term with two meanings in academic life, signaling both an end and a beginning. You recently attended your high school graduation in celebration of the award of your hard-earned diploma and the beginning of adult life. Similarly, four years hence, you will attend another commencement ceremony to receive your college degree and to move forward through worlds beyond and as yet unknown. Replete with colorful gowns, ritual steeped in academic tradition, and the stirring sounds of trumpets, the college commencement ceremony is a glorious rite of passage. The college gates open again, faculty move from the lead, and, if you have been diligent, you will march through them as an educated mind. Commencement is a fanfare both for your achievement and for the endless possibility of human endeavor.

Soon you will enter college. One day you will leave it. Do not miss a minute in between—eyes, ears, heart, and mind wide open.

ABOUT THE AUTHOR

John T. Kirkpatrick earned his B.A. at Colby College and his Ph.D. in Sociology at the University of New Hampshire. He is Associate Dean of the College of Liberal Arts, Research Associate Professor of Sociology, and Director of Justiceworks at the University of New Hampshire. He has worked with first-year college students for twenty years.